BROKEN

THE UNDERDOG

A SERIES BY

Jakyrannee Phillips

BROKEN

Jakyrannee Phillips

BROKEN
Published by Jakyrannee Phillips

ISBN-13: 978-1548534233

ISBN-10: 1548534234

Cover Designed by Danielle Alysse Martin

All glory to God for giving me the courage to write this story. Also, to my mother, mentors, and family for the prayers and motivation to keep going.

Foreword

In the fall of 2015, I met a young lady from Monroe, LA while attending an orientation at Tougaloo College. The orientation was for the Destination Graduation Mentoring Program. My desire was to mentor a freshman student. I wanted to provide support to that student as they matriculated through college. The amazing young person introduced to me was Jakyrannee Phillips. I couldn't have imagined that my life would change after meeting her. It is a privilege and an honor to know her, but more so to celebrate in her many accomplishments. When I met her, one of her greatest desires was to write a book. It is a blessing to see this desire manifest.

I encourage you to embrace each page of this book. This young lady has passion, drive, determination and outstanding faith. She is an overcomer. She walks by faith, and not by sight. Despite life's obstacles, she has decided to press through to what she sees as her God given path to prosperity. She puts her feelings out there for others to view as she moves from a place of opposition to victory. Welcome to the story of her life. There are many life situations and circumstances that impact our lives. Life's challenges can become barriers, hindrances, and even boulders to keep us from the purpose and destiny ordained by God. We all have experienced things that leave us broken. If handled correctly, being broken can also be a place of growth and strength to catapult you to victory.

Can you imagine taking life by the horns as a college student to conquer your dreams? Well, this young lady has done so. I support her in her many endeavors. This is just the beginning. As her foundational scripture states, *"A man's gift maketh room for him, and bringeth him before great men."* Her gift has undoubtedly made room for her. Trust and believe that God has called Jaykrannee Phillips to accomplish great things. She is stamped with

Proverbs 10:22 which states, *"The blessing of the Lord, it maketh rich, and he addeth no sorrow with it."*

Jakyrannee, I love you and thank God for you.

Wendy Mahoney, Mentor
"He healeth the broken in heart, and bindeth up their wounds." Psalms 147:3

Table of Contents

Introduction

"She will never be anything!"
"Watch she get pregnant in high school and drop out like the rest!"

Those words were literally spoken about me. If I had believed those words, I wouldn't be where I am today. Today, I am the CEO of *Broken Girls Magazine*. I am also in the process of publishing my first book. I was always taught that hurting people hurt other people. I have lived that unfortunate truth.

On the inside, I was always so angry and pissed off at the world. I felt as if nothing was ever going right in my life. The people I thought were supposed to be supporting me weren't. And, as we say now, it made me "feel some type of way". In the midst of going through everything and feeling that way, God replaced what I was lacking with what I needed. He placed people in my life to help guide and train me to become who he wanted me to be.

It hasn't been easy. I would often get discouraged. It was so easy to fall back into the things I used to do in the past. I learned that in order to change my situation, I had to change my mindset. I decided that I was not going to live paycheck to paycheck. I was not going to get a degree from school to make thousands and only be satisfied with that. Proverbs 18:16 says, *"A man's gift maketh room for him, and bringeth him before great men."* I knew I was born a millionaire and that wealth was placed inside of me. It was time for to give birth to that very fact.

No one ever told me it was ok to be mad. Instead, I used that energy to do what I was passionate about. Along the way, I learned that I would lose people that I thought would have remained with me for a lifetime. I keep God first in everything. I know he will never fail me. God is always on time. He knows what I want before I say a word. Now I know when I ask God for something, he has to prepare me to receive whatever it might be. With all being said, I encourage you not to give up on your dreams. Keep going! You could be right at the finish line and not know it. It took me five years to give birth to this project. That is because I complained daily. I would become discouraged, worrying about how I was going to finance everything. But all God wanted me to do was write. He had already taken care of everything. Someone is waiting on you in order for them to go to the next level. They need what God has placed on the inside of you. You don't deserve everything you're going through. However, you're going through it to be a light to someone else. Are you going to give birth to that thing? Or, will you continue to complain about what isn't right?

Chapter One
A Voiceless Child

Dear Diary,

Am I not skinny enough to be accepted for all of the different talents I have?

Society trying to tell me I'm too thick and too smart to have this image on the outside.

Too curvy with a fat ass they say, slim waste, round face, not built like most but blessed with something I didn't have to go out and buy.

I get tired of hearing what I look like on the outside every day. I look at myself in the mirror 24 hours a day, and seven days a week ...

Stop judging me by my outside appearance and take your time to really get to know me.

Who I am goes beyond my image.

What's wrong with me? No what's wrong with you?

Sincerely,

A Broken Girl

It takes a bold woman to open herself up completely to the world, revealing any and everything she ever experienced in a lifetime. There would be some people who would need the answer she has on the inside of her. However, she is also afraid of the those who would take her story and make fun of it. She endures sleepless nights because she knows she can no longer keep the answer on the inside of her. Thoughts and dreams constantly interrupt her, telling her to give birth to purpose. The question of whether or not she has what it takes to restore people stays on her mind. How she wishes she could just forget about the rumors, the what ifs, and everything else. She just wants to let it all out. At night she can hear voices whispering in her ear. The voices exclaim that they are waiting on her to tell her story so that they can be free. Her biggest fear is not doing what she's supposed to do in the time it's supposed to be done.

She knows that she didn't deserve some of the things

that she's experienced. She also knows that she went through for someone else. She's thankful that someone was obedient and gave birth to the answer she needed to go forth. She now wants to continue on with this race by doing what needs to be done.

Can you imagine growing up only being known for your outside appearance? When someone is asked how they know me, the most common response is, "The girl with the fat ass? Yeah, I know her." Every time I would hear that answer it would take something from me. I couldn't walk down the streets without older men trying to get at me. A lot of men would try to give me smooth conversations. They said they would give me the world if I belonged to them. As I've gotten older, I felt like I got judged the hardest. If I was to wear something fitted, I would be told to cover up because I was too thick. It always seemed like nothing I wore was ever good enough. I would feel worthless and uncomfortable all the time. I constantly felt like I wasn't anything but the body image that everyone wanted to have. It was automatically assumed that I was having a sexual relationship with any guy I had a conversation with.

I would always hear, "Girl where did you get your body from. Can I touch it?" Irritated by the different conversations, I would find something to do that would help me forget about everything that was going on around me. I wanted people to see that it was more to me than my outside appearance. Writing has always been my escape from the world. I would always write about whatever I felt or experienced because my pen and paper was my voice.

I always paid attention to the things that went on around me. Those things consisted of problems at school, adult conversations, different types of relationship altercations, and more. Seeing some of the things that I did made me want to help people. I would pray and ask God to take me through things so that I can have a story to write that would be the answer to someone's problem.

I would always hear people talk about God and all the things he had done for them. I wanted to have the same experience they had had, or at least something close to it. It wasn't long after, that I started to experience the things for which I asked. In that time, I didn't know that when you ask God for something, you have to be specific. Also, you have to make room to receive it. By saying yes, there's a price that you have to pay. That price can cause you to lose family, friends, and much more... but for a good cause.

I started experiencing things that weren't normal for a young girl to experience at the time. I found myself doing things I said I would never do, and going places I said I would never go. My body started developing into this nice figure that caused me to look older than I actually was. Constantly battling with the hurt from family, friends, and the world, I wanted to be free. I wanted to be free from feeling like I had to depend on anybody for anything. If I had to make ends meet, I would make it happen. I always said I would n ever sleep with a man for money or put myself in a position to get a sexually transmitted disease. Later, I learned that you should never say what you wouldn't do until you actually get in that position because it's not so easy, especially if you are going through hard times.

I didn't have many friends because a lot of girls would secretly envy me from the attention I was getting. I became coldhearted after dealing with a lot of toxic relationships from boys and girls. I went out for revenge for everybody who ever hurt me because I wanted them to feel the pain they caused me. I started persuading my friends at the time to do things they said they would never do. Also, my love for receiving fast money grew and I became addicted to sex. I knew the lifestyle I was living wasn't right but I didn't care either because I felt like nobody cared about me. I thought giving my life to God would protect me from going through hard trials, but it seemed as if it only got worse. It was so bad to the point where I felt like committing suicide. However, I wasn't crazy enough to actually do it. At the time, I was being set up on purpose. I was experiencing everything I did to help young girls who are constantly seeking that love and attention from the wrong people. As I talk you through my journey step by step, I want you to take everything you can from it and know that trouble don't last always.

Chapter Two
Bloodlines

I was the baby girl of four siblings, then the middle child of six when I was blessed with twin sisters on my mother's side. Before the twins came along, I was raised under one roof with my three siblings. I saw a few of my siblings on my dad side. However, not all of them wanted any dealings with me. Some felt as if my father shouldn't have had any more children after them.

I always wanted good relationships with my siblings on both sides. Who doesn't want to have a big brother or a big sister? At one point, I wanted to be like my friends. They were able to talk to their older siblings about any and everything. Unfortunately, it wasn't like that with me.

Even though I was the baby at the time, I felt like the oldest on my mom's side. I would get in trouble for everything. Even if an argument broke out with one of my older siblings and I didn't start it, I still got in trouble. I always felt like I was the different, but special one. When I say special, it is because I knew I would be the chosen one to help change my family name in a major way. I would get talked about for staying in my room most of the time at home. Relatives would jokingly say I was suffering from depression and other mental issues. Little did they know, those things were actually true.

I suffered those things because I always desired to have a close bond with my parents and siblings. My relationship wasn't where I wanted it to be with my mother. On top of that, it seemed as if the other siblings were getting all of her attention when she was at home. There would be places I wanted to go with friends. I wasn't allowed to go. If another sibling were to ask, they would be able to go with their friends. My mother was very strict about how things went in her house. If you ask her something and she gives you an answer, that's the end of the conversation. It's best if you not ask her again.

Due to me not having the freedom I wanted, which was to go out with friends and stay the night at others house, I would stay in my room and journal about my days. I would write about my family, friends, and teachers if they made me mad. Many times, I would come home from school and my family would have found my journals. I can remember getting so mad because I would hide my journals before I left. But some way, they would go find and find them.

I always felt as if I was in competition with my siblings. They would get recognized for the things they were doing in and outside of school, but no one ever paid attention to little ole me. I felt this way but never knew how to come out and openly talk about it. I felt that if I were to express my feelings about how I felt, I would get laughed at and talked about. I love all of my siblings from the bottom of my heart, even if we are never as close as I want us to be.

My family wasn't big like the families you see on TV. I barely knew my relatives because growing up, there were only certain family members we would be allowed to go around for whatever reason. We didn't attend reunions on a regular basis. Therefore, I had no clue as to who I was related to. I always wanted to grow up knowing who my relatives where.

At the age of sixteen, I was finally able to call myself a big sister. My mother had beautiful twin girls that I always wanted. I wanted to have someone who could look up to me. I could tell them everything I went through so that they wouldn't experience as much as I did.

Chapter Three
The Overachiever

From elementary to high school I was considered a troubled teen. I would act out in class and get into multiple altercations for the smallest things. I can remember being so angry and mad that I didn't care what I did, what I said, or if I would even get in trouble. I would always get into fights with other students and be disrespectful to my teachers. Every time a teacher said something to me, I would have a smart remark to say. I would even challenge them with my eyes. I always had good grades in school. I was an honor student from elementary school to high school. I was inducted into the Beta club, graduated high school in three years, and was Valedictorian of my class. I became involved in sports and organizations just to have something to do, hoping it would fill a void and give me the attention I wanted. I would get close to my teachers on purpose. That would result in me being called a teacher's pet by others students. My teachers cared for me. They always encouraged me to chase my dreams and do what I love. I would love being under them so much that I would stay hours after school just so I wouldn't have to go home. It wasn't that my home was a bad place. I just knew I would have to go back into my dark place.

Chapter Four
The Letter She Wrote

Dear Mama,

Mama can you hear me?

Why don't you understand me?

You see me every day, but never pay attention to me.

I'm supposed to be your baby girl, but this silence is killing me. Afraid to tell you how I really feel, thinking you will disown me. All I want you to do is ask me if I'm ok!

We should go shopping from time to time, just so I can see your face. I rarely see you anymore, but I bet you don't care. I want that motherly love from my mother, not anyone else.

Hurting so badly on the inside, it seems like I'm losing myself. Stressing every day, feeling like I'm coming closer to my death. You say hurtful things toward me which always replay in my head. Having me thinking negative things about you, wishing you were dead.

That's crazy I know, because I would miss you so much.

Mama please talk to me. I'm going through so much. How can I miss something I never had? I don't know. I guess I daydream too much. I'm never losing hope on us mama. I promise you when I say this stuff. I feel as if I'm in this alone, crying out for help to anyone around but I'm going to always smile. I refuse to let anyone see me down. When I'm all alone, I go through this stage again. I just want to be in your presence and hear you call me your baby girl again. Mama, can you hear me now?

— A Hurting Child

My mother was a hard-working woman. She would go to work early in the morning and sleep in at night. I would hate to see her come in the house tired. That meant we wouldn't be able to do anything. I always told myself that I would make a good amount of money to take care of her. I wanted her to get some rest and not have to get up and work long hours anymore. Sometimes she would even pick up a second job just to make sure my siblings and I had food to eat and a place to stay. My mother would always read books. She would take my older siblings and I to library from time to time. That's how I began reading books and writing as well. She would always make us go get a book to read. She had books all around the house as well and bookshelves in my room. At night, I would sneak and read some of her books, hoping I wouldn't get caught. She would always know when someone been on her shelf.

My mother was very strict. I wasn't allowed to do the things that other children my age were allowed to do. I couldn't go to parties or attend sleepovers. When I would ask if I could go to a friend's house, she would respond by saying, "What friend? I'm your friend. You don't have any friends." Just as I wasn't allowed to go over their house, they weren't allowed to come to mine. Her favorite thing to say was, "Because I'm the mama and you're the child." I would get so mad that I would go in my room, shut the door, and cry. I was staying in the house with the woman who gave birth to me. But I felt as if she didn't even know me. I would get my journal and write hurtful things. I never did understand why she raised me the way she did until I got older.

I was actually glad that my mother didn't let me go to that party or friend's house. Each time, someone would get shot that night or get into a fight and go to jail. All I knew was that I wanted to get out of the house. I did not know she was only protecting me for my own good. When I was around fifteen, I got tired of not being able to go places. I started sneaking out of the house to have the freedom I wanted. My mother always locked her door at eleven. So, sometimes I would open my room window only to come back and it be locked. During that time, I became very disrespectful and disobedient towards my mother. I was tired of her and her rules. Every time I would ask her something she would respond with something I didn't want to hear. I would be pissed off to the point to where I was actually ready to fight her. I would think about the freedom my other siblings had, and I grew tired of being sheltered. I was fifteen and I felt grown enough to make my own decisions. I came and went as I pleased. My mother eventually got tired of it and put me out her house. I stayed with my grandmother until college. I always loved my grandmother because I was able to do whatever I wanted. I was able to talk to my grandmother about things I couldn't talk to others about. It got to a point to where I would get along with my mother as long as I didn't stay with her. I know I hurt her and wanted to make up for it. But I knew there was no use trying to make things better. I started to pray for our relationship. I asked God to soften her heart and help us have the mother and daughter relationship I wanted. Of course, it didn't happen overnight. But as days went on, we've grew closer.

Later, I learned that God turned everything around and made it work together for my good. Everything I went through and experienced with my mother was necessary. It gave me the strength to go hard and never give up. Even though my mother wasn't around, she supported me in her own way. Whenever I told her I wanted to do something, she would say, "Baby you can do whatever you want." That's all I wanted to hear. All I wanted was to make my mother proud. I wanted her to know she didn't fail as a parent and because of her tough love, I am the unstoppable woman I am today. I would often look at her and wonder how she would react if I were to tell her the places I had been or what I had been doing. A part of me was ashamed and scared she might disown me. If she did, I wouldn't blame her.

Chapter 5
A Father's Presence

I didn't grow up in a house with my father. I didn't wake up to him every day. I still don't know what actually happened with him and my mother. To be honest, I don't care to find out. I do know that all I ever wanted was my daddy. I wanted to receive those weekly phone calls and messages that I would hear my friends discuss. Unlike them, I wasn't able to call my father, ask for anything and get it within ten minutes because my parents didn't have it like that.

I would see and talk to my father twice a year. At that time, a lot of children my age hated their father because he wasn't active in their life. I didn't. I was always a daddy's girl at heart. To others it was strange that I would talk about my father who I rarely ever saw due to him staying in a different state. But I didn't care.

My father was a football player, and was very confident. Every time I would talk to him, he would tell me to put my all into whatever it is I was doing. Since we were both athletes, he always related sports to life situations. That's one reason why I cared for him so much.

Although we had good conversations, I wish he would have been around more. I always felt that if my father was around to teach me about relationships and friendships, I wouldn't have done some of the embarrassing things I've done, that I was once shame to talk about.

Also, I would always see young girls doing the daughter and father dance. I knew I would never get that opportunity because my father stayed thousands miles away. I'm nineteen now and have never given up on the thought of having that dance with my father.

Chapter Six
But I Loved Him

Have you ever dated someone you thought you would be with forever? You didn't care what anyone said about him because you knew he was the one. He was the one you hoped to someday marry, who would become the father to your children. We all had that "him" before Mine was named Rodney.

Rodney was the man of my dreams at the time. Nobody could say anything that would make me leave him. He was very well built and taller than me, just how I like the guys I date. His teeth were white as snow and perfect with no gaps. Rodney worked at a warehouse. He got paid every week and made more money than I did in a month. He had his own car, which was paid off, and a nice apartment with plenty of furniture.

I wasn't accustomed to dating a guy who was the

same age as me who seemingly had it all together. I would always get into fights with my mother because she wanted me to leave him alone. She didn't know him like I knew him. She got tired of me coming in late and leaving home all the time. She said he was no good. But it didn't stop me from being with him. Eventually, she kicked me out the house.

I didn't care about being kicked out of the house because he always told me his house would be my second home. The first week I stayed with Rodney, I thought my mother would call me back home. She didn't. Rodney would fix me breakfast every morning before he left for work, ran my bath water, and made sure I had everything I needed. I was working part time at Mc Donald's, but he made me quit. He said no woman of his would ever have to work. I would get up every morning to wash the dishes and making sure the house was clean. I would iron his clothes for work, making sure they were starched down with creases in them. Then, I would sit and ask myself how in the hell I got myself into this position. I was not even married to this man but acting as if he was my husband. I didn't have many friends. But I did have one friend named Chasidy. She hated Rodney. She thought he was very controlling. She also suspected that Rodney was cheating on me. However, I didn't care to hear that because every night he would come home to me, and that's all that really mattered.

Chasidy been my friend for 5 years, we met in the fourth grade and have been close ever since. He would never like me to be around her. He said she was messy and that I didn't need those types of friends around me. I knew the real reason he didn't like her was because she didn't want me with him.

My love for Rodney was so strong because he had been there for me since I was a junior High School. When I needed new clothes or my phone bill paid, he took care of that for me. It was hard to break away from somebody like that. In the back of my mind, I felt as though I would never find someone else to take care of me like that. For that reason, I kept holding on to that relationship. Weeks went by and Rodney started coming home late. He said they were giving him more hours because his company had gotten busy with sales.

He would leave me money for food and to shop with. I never questioned him being busy with work. Well, that was until I found out his secret. I was doing laundry one day and found test results in his pocket. He had been tested for Chlamydia and the results were positive. Mad as hell, I stormed into the bedroom going through his personal items. I destroyed everything. I couldn't believe he had been cheating on me and brought something back to me. I never imagined I would have an STD, and especially from this person who constantly said he loved me and would never hurt me. Digging deeper into his belongings, I found a picture of him and this dark skin girl. She had hazel eyes and long brown hair that stopped in the middle of her back. She had dimples deeper than any I ever seen. She was actually very pretty.

Tears started rolling down my face as I noticed them holding hands and smiling. Not only that, but they also had a baby girl sitting in between them. The word "family" was written at the bottom. In my head, I was wondering where in the hell that came from. How was I so blind and in love with him that I never knew about this? He was out there messing around on me and had a hidden family as well. Deep down inside, I wanted to kill the baby mother, and the other chic too. I was supposed to be the mother of his child. I sacrificed so much to be with him. My mother hated me and I couldn't go back home. I broke almost everything in that man's house. I had to find somewhere to go quickly.

I searched for my phone in between the couch

cushions. When I found it, I dialed Chasidy's number. Crying and unable to speak, I just held the phone. After getting myself together, I told her to come get me quick and fast. It was 9 o'clock on the dot and I knew he would be home in thirty minutes. I packed a few clothes so it wouldn't be obvious that I wasn't coming back. I had been saving all of the money he had been giving me. Therefore, I could just go buy what I needed. I grabbed my charger out the wall. Turning to leave out of the house, I see Rodney standing in the doorway watching me. I was scared as hell but I didn't want him to know. I spoke and tried to brush past him. He slapped me so hard in my face that everything fell out of my hand. He got on top of me and beat me as if I was some stranger on the street. Laying there in disbelief and screaming out for help, I knew no one would hear me. My phone was going off. I knew it was Chasidy calling. However, it was too late. I knew he was about to beat the hell out of me all night. There was no escaping because I was in too deep. All I could think about was that I should have listened to my mama. I stayed because I thought we were in love. Well, at least I know I loved him.

Chapter Seven
The Underdog

As I said earlier, I was considered an underdog. I was overlooked and looked down on. People always told me that better days were coming. For me, that was actually true. It wasn't necessarily safe though. My life took a path of its own. I actually enjoyed the lifestyle I was living. I was getting the attention, affection, and money I wanted without stress. I started blocking out everything negative in my life. This included family and friends, or anybody. I always said I would live my life to the fullest. That's exactly what I did. I walked around with dark personal secrets on the inside. In the beginning, I was afraid of what people would say and how the world would view me. Because of that, I kept quiet about what I've witnessed and experienced. I would walk around smiling and laughing, but behind it all was the other part of me that I hid for years. One thing I hid was that I discovered I had an STD my freshman year of high school. I received the treatments for it, and it was cleared. I cried and cried because I always heard people talking about the girls that had STD'S. I always said I would never get one. After that happened, I started talking to multiple boys and using them. I wanted them to feel the hurt I felt. I wanted them to experience what I had been through. Also, if you couldn't support me financially, I wasn't interested. Later, I met some girls that became close friends. We have all been through some of the same things. We decided to take it to the next level. On the weekend, we would go roam the streets and talk to older men. They would give us more money than what we had been receiving. We did that for about five months, but stopped when they wanted us to start sleeping with them. I would think about doing it all the time. However, I was always afraid. Being afraid only lasted until reality kicked in and I realized I wasn't getting anything out of my parents' pockets anymore. I was supposed to have everything together. But in reality, I didn't. I introduced this lifestyle to every female that became attached to me. We all started running things everywhere we went. It soon became our new hustle. It was more like a drug or our own personal high. All we needed was a shot of Patron, and let's just say the rest was history.

About the Author

Jakyrannee Phillips is a Mass Communication major at the Prestigious Tougaloo College in Tougaloo, MS. Phillips is 19 years of age from the Sportsman Paradise of Monroe, Louisiana. At the age of seventeen, she graduated from Vision Academy. Phillips graduated in three years, and was Valedictorian of her class. While attending Vision Academy, she participated in multiple organizations and held various leadership roles. She was president of FCA and captain of the Varsity Girls Basketball team. She was a member of the Entrepreneurship Team, Prom Committee, and many more.

Phillips began writing at the age of ten. Then, she decided she would write and publish books. Writing is one of the things that she is passionate about most. She would always write about whatever she experienced, or witnessed other people around her go through.

Growing up, she was always the underdog. While going through what she experienced, she didn't understand what was going on. But she knew her testimony in the form of short stories would help others. She also enjoys dancing, being creative, and empowering others with her smile and wild personality. As of now, Phillips' has her own magazine titled *Broken Girls Magazine*, t-shirt line, book she wrote called *Broken*, and is a part of a collaboration book with Mississippi authors titled *Purpose the New Voice of Mississippi Authors.* She is a Mary Kay Consultant all while being a full-time college student. Phillips believes "The question is not who's going to let me, but who's going to stop me?" She also believes by putting God first in everything daily, ANYTHING is possible.

Jakyrannee Phillips

Made in the USA
Columbia, SC
06 October 2024